How Birds Fly

BY RUSSELL FREEDMAN

drawings by Lorence F. Bjorklund

HOLIDAY HOUSE • New York

For VERNON IVES

Text copyright © 1977 by Russell Freedman
Illustrations copyright © 1977 by Lorence F. Bjorklund
All rights reserved
Printed in the United States of America

Library of Congress Cataloging in Publication Data

Freedman, Russell.
  How birds fly.

  Includes index.
  1. Flight—Juvenile literature.   I. Bjorklund,
Lorence F.   II. Title.
QL698.7.F73   598.2′1′852   77-555
ISBN 0-8234-0301-7

Contents

Author's Note

The flapping flight of birds is not fully understood even today. Birds and airplanes are subject to the same laws of aerodynamics, and yet the rigid wing of a plane is simple indeed compared with the flapping wing of a bird. So many complex forces act upon a beating wing that it may never be possible to define them all. However, many principles of flapping flight have been discovered, mainly through high-speed photography. And we know a great deal about birds' gliding flight, which is much like that of an airplane.

This book is intended as a simple introduction for those who may have wondered how a bird stays up, how it uses its wings, and how it maneuvers. Much of the material here is based on *The Flight of Birds,* by John H. Storer (Cranbrook Institute of Science, Bulletin No. 28, 1948), which includes many still photographs from motion picture films and is an essential source for the serious student of bird flight. An excellent review of Storer's study and more recent findings can be found in chapters 1, 3, and 21 of the standard text, *The Life of Birds,* by Joel Carl Welty (W. B. Saunders & Co., 2nd Edition, 1975). Hovering flight is explained fully in *Hummingbirds,* by Crawford H. Greenewalt (Doubleday, 1960). Technical aspects of aerodynamics are covered in *The Science of Flight,* by O. G. Sutton (Penguin Books, 1955). For the general reader, detailed but less technical accounts include *Birds in Flight,* by John Kaufmann (Morrow, 1970), and *The Miracle of Flight,* by Richard Cromer (Doubleday, 1968).

A sea gull flies overhead. Beating its wings, it climbs higher and higher toward the sun. Then it levels off and glides in a slow circle with its wings spread wide. What holds the gull up? What happens when a bird flies?

Feathers for Flying

These birds are too young to fly. Before they can lift themselves into the sky, they need strong muscles and long flight feathers.

When a bird hatches, it has no flight feathers. It starts life with soft, fluffy feathers called *down.* Some newly hatched birds, like ducklings, have a thick, warm coat of down. Others, like songbirds, have just a few wispy down feathers. They keep warm by snuggling beneath their mother or father.

newly hatched robin

newly hatched duckling

young American robin

young Pekin duck

As a bird grows up, it gets its first coat of *contour feathers*. These new feathers are smooth and stiff. They cover the bird's head, body, tail, and wings. The widest contour feathers are in the tail. The longest are in the bird's wings.

Beneath their contour feathers, many grown birds have a coat of down next to their skin, like a warm set of underwear. Smooth contour feathers on top and fluffy down feathers beneath make up most of a bird's body covering.

7

down feather   *contour feather*

Long contour feathers in a bird's wings are called *flight feathers.* A flight feather is light enough to float in a breeze and strong enough to bend without breaking. Though it looks simple, it has millions of carefully fitted parts. The feather is held together by a stiff stem, or *shaft.* At the end of the shaft is a hollow *quill,* fastened to the bird's skin. On each side of the shaft is a thin *web,* made of hundreds of slender strips called *barbs.* Jutting out from each barb are many tiny hooks, too small to be seen without a microscope. These hooks work like zippers. When the wind ruffles a feather and separates the webs, the bird can "zip" them back together. It simply runs its beak along the webs and smooths the feather out.

WEBS

Each web has about 600 barbs.

SHAFT

BARB

Each barb has hundreds of tiny hooks that work like zippers.

BARBS

SHAFT

QUILL

flight feather from wing

gannet

"Contour" means outline. Contour feathers give a bird its smooth, sleek outline, or shape. Like an airplane, a bird is streamlined to cut easily through the air. Its body tapers smoothly from beak to tail. The feathers lie flat, so air slides over them. As a bird flies, it folds its legs tightly against its belly. Nothing sticks out to drag against the air, not even ears. The opening to each ear is hidden beneath the head feathers.

A Lightweight Body

Beneath its coat of feathers, a bird's body is much smaller than you might think. It is designed to weigh as little as possible. Inside the body are bubble-like spaces filled with air. These *air sacs* are attached to the bird's lungs and branch throughout its body, even into some bones. They help cool the body as the bird breathes, and they cut down on the bird's weight.

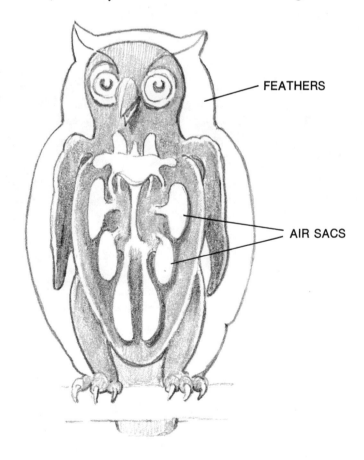

FEATHERS

AIR SACS

Light weight is important to any creature that flies. One of the heaviest of all flying birds, the trumpeter swan, weighs just 25 to 30 pounds. A bald eagle weighs only 11 or 12 pounds. Most birds are much smaller. A full-grown robin weighs about 3 ounces. A sparrow weighs one ounce.

A bird also has a lightweight skeleton, built of bones that are thin but very strong. Many of the bones are hollow. Some are strengthened inside by stiff struts. The skull is made of paper-thin sheets of bone fused together. The large breast-bone supports the powerful flight muscles that move the bird's wings. Some birds have a skeleton that weighs less than their feathers.

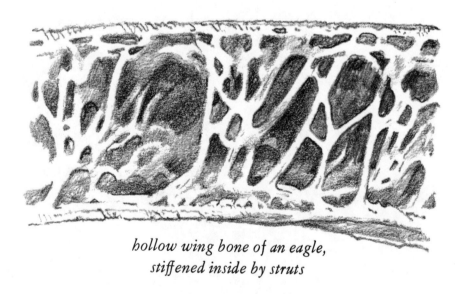

hollow wing bone of an eagle,
stiffened inside by struts

BREASTBONE

skeleton of a gull

Wings

California condor

The bones in a bird's wing are very much like the bones in a human arm. The bird has an upper arm between the shoulder and elbow, a lower arm between the elbow and wrist, and a hand. It is in the hand section that a bird is most different from us. A bird's hand is longer and narrower than a human hand when compared with the rest of its arm. A bird's hand also has fewer bones, with just two fingers and a thumb. The finger bones are joined together, so the bird cannot move them. However, it can open and close its thumb.

14

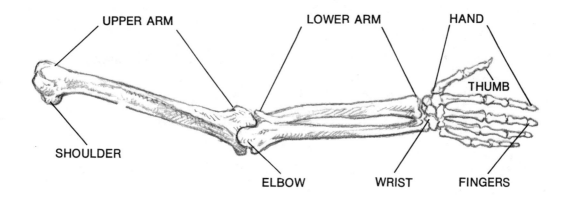

UPPER ARM   LOWER ARM   HAND

THUMB

SHOULDER

ELBOW   WRIST   FINGERS

human arm bones

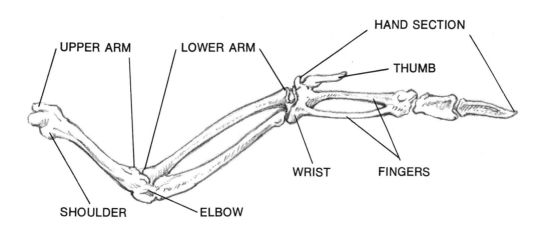

UPPER ARM   LOWER ARM   HAND SECTION

THUMB

WRIST   FINGERS

SHOULDER   ELBOW

bird's wing bones

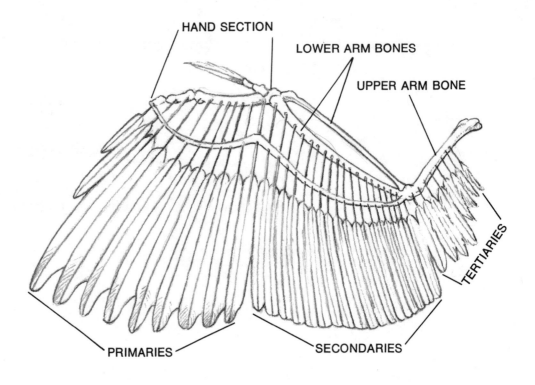

HAND SECTION

LOWER ARM BONES

UPPER ARM BONE

TERTIARIES

PRIMARIES

SECONDARIES

Anchored to the wing bones are long flight feathers. The longest flight feathers, called *primaries,* are attached to the hand section. Most birds have ten primaries on each wing. The *secondaries* are not quite as long. They are attached to the lower arm bones. The number of secondaries depends on the length of the bird's wing. Other feathers, called *tertiaries* (TER-she-air-eez), close the gap between the elbow and shoulder. A bird can bend its wings at the shoulder, the elbow, and the wrist.

Flight Muscles

A bird's biggest and strongest muscles are the chest muscles that move its wings. Long before a young bird starts to fly, it exercises these *flight muscles.* Every day it stretches and beats its wings. Soon it is able to rise a few feet into the air. It flaps hard, then drops back down again.

young red-shouldered hawk

Flight muscles are attached to the breastbone, or *keel*. The outer set of muscles lowers the wings, while the inner set raises them. The lowering muscles are bigger, because a bird must work harder when it pulls its wings down.

Some young birds stop eating a day or so before their first flight. They seem to lose their appetites. This may be a bird's way of losing weight before finally testing its wings. If the nest is in a tree, the parents may fly back and forth, calling

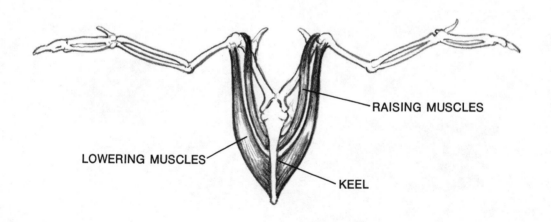

RAISING MUSCLES

LOWERING MUSCLES

KEEL

out to the young one. The fledgling climbs to the edge of the nest and looks down. Suddenly it jumps. It pulls up its legs, stretches its neck, beats its wings, and flies. Some young birds fly easily their first time out. Others seem to need quite a lot of practice.

fledgling golden eagle

How Birds and Planes Are Lifted

Many people think that a bird must flap its wings to stay in the air, but this is not the case. A bird can stay up without flapping its wings, just as an airplane does. Birds and planes stay up in the same way. They are lifted by air rushing past their wings.

A simple experiment will show how a wing is lifted. Hold a piece of paper by one edge, so the loose end droops toward the floor. Remember that the paper is surrounded by air. Air presses against it from all sides. Air pushes down against the top of the paper just as hard as air pushes up against the bottom.

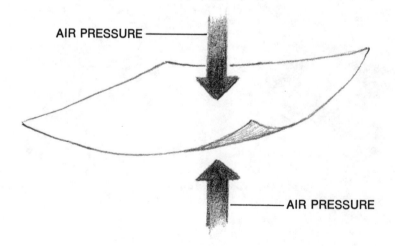

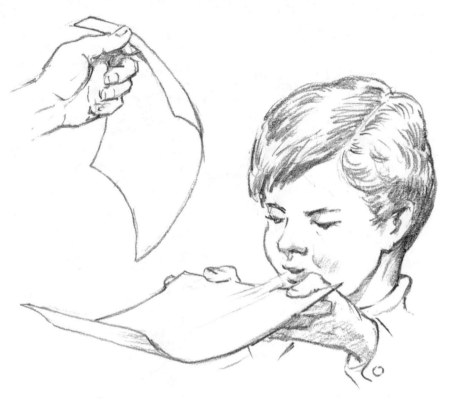

Now blow over the top of the paper. What happens? It flies upward! The paper rises because the air on top is moving faster than the air below. When air flows faster past the paper or any surface, it does not press down as hard as before. The faster the air moves, the less it presses against the paper. In fact, as the air on top speeds up, it tends to pull away and suck the paper upward.

By blowing over the paper, you have reduced the air pressure on top without changing the air pressure below. The air below continues to push up against the bottom of the paper. Now the paper is being *pushed from below* and *pulled from above*. It flies upward because these two forces together are stronger than the pull of gravity.

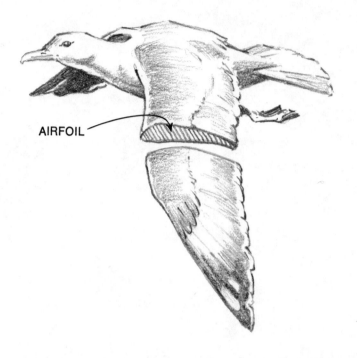

AIRFOIL

The same kind of air movement that lifted the paper also lifts a bird's wings. A wing is designed to make air flow faster over the top, just as air flowed faster over the top of the paper.

If you cut through a wing, as shown above, you can see how the wing is shaped. Notice that the top surface of the wing is curved more than the bottom surface. The greater curve on top is important, because it affects the way that air flows over the wing. In order to get past the steep curve, the air on top must speed up. It moves faster than air flowing beneath the wing. This special curved shape is called an *airfoil*. It is the shape of a bird's wing and a plane's wing too.

22

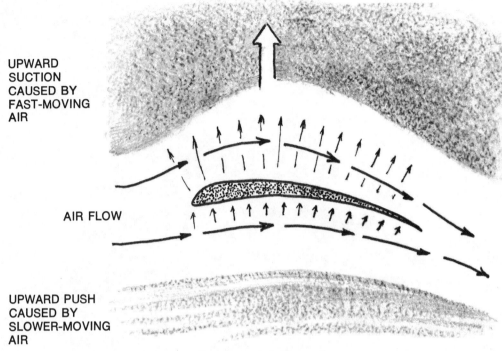

LIFT

UPWARD
SUCTION
CAUSED BY
FAST-MOVING
AIR

AIR FLOW

UPWARD PUSH
CAUSED BY
SLOWER-MOVING
AIR

how an airfoil works

This diagram shows what happens when a wing with an airfoil shape cuts through the air. As air hits the steeper curve on top, it speeds up. This fast-moving air tends to pull away from the top of the wing, just as it pulled away from the top of the paper. Pulling away causes suction. The wing is sucked upward, as if by a giant vacuum cleaner. Below the wing, air flows more slowly. This slower air presses up against the bottom of the wing. The wing is pushed from below by air pressure and pulled from above by suction. Pressure and suction working together are called *lift*. And lift is what holds a bird or plane in the sky.

23

How a Bird Gets More Lift

killdeer

Lift is caused by air speeding past a bird's wings. The faster the air rushes over the tops of the wings, the more lifting power the wings will have. The more slowly the air flows over the wings, the less lifting power they will have. To get more lift, a slow-flying bird tilts its wings, so that the front of each wing is facing upward. As the wing tilts, air flowing over the wing speeds up greatly. Faster-moving air causes more suction above the wing. The wing is pulled from above with greater force, so the amount of lift is greater. The angle at which the wing faces the oncoming air is called the *angle of attack*.

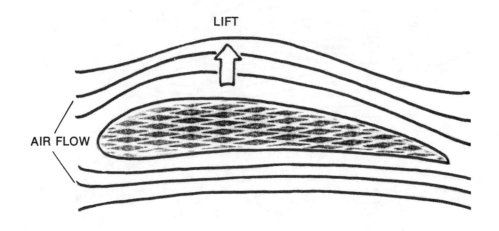

LIFT

AIR FLOW

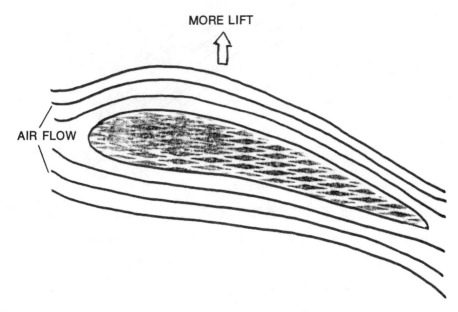

MORE LIFT

AIR FLOW

angle of attack: as the wing tilts upward,
air moves faster over the top of the wing.

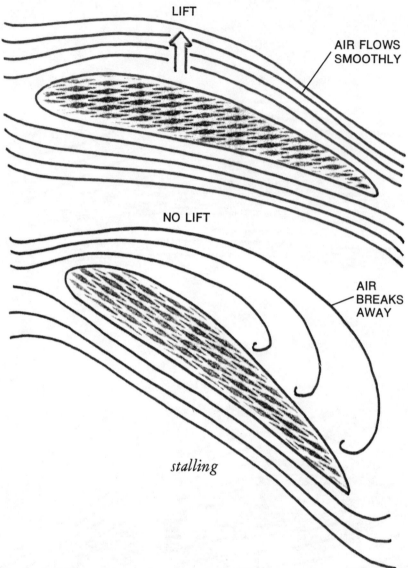

LIFT

AIR FLOWS
SMOOTHLY

NO LIFT

AIR
BREAKS
AWAY

stalling

A bird can tilt its wings only so far. If it tilts them too high, air can no longer flow smoothly over the wing tops. Instead, the air will break away and swirl around. All lift will suddenly disappear, and the bird will *stall*. If it stalls, it will start falling toward earth.

26

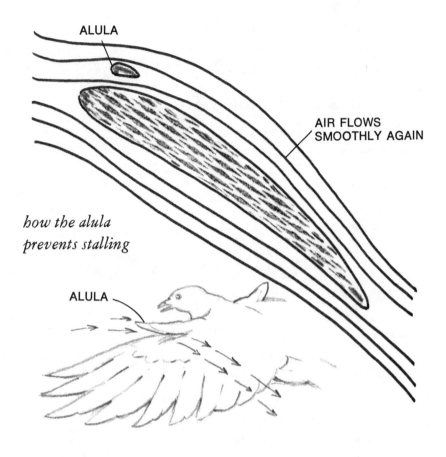

ALULA

AIR FLOWS
SMOOTHLY AGAIN

*how the alula
prevents stalling*

ALULA

To keep from stalling, the bird has special slots in its wings that open and close. One of these slots is formed by a little wing, called the *alula*, which is attached to the thumb bone. When the alula opens, air squeezes through the narrow slot between the alula and the rest of the wing. The air speeds up and starts flowing smoothly again. Instead of stalling, the bird now has more lift than before. Other slots, formed by flight feathers in the wing tips, help keep slow-flying birds in the air.

27

How a Bird Moves Forward: Flapping Flight

FORWARD MOTION

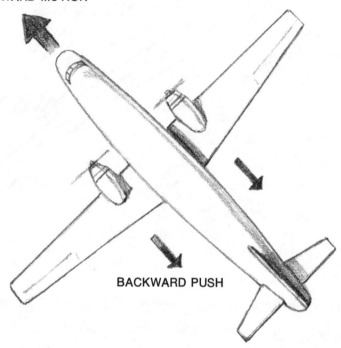

BACKWARD PUSH

In order to be lifted by its wings, a bird or plane must be moving forward fast enough to make air rush past the wings. A plane is driven through the air by its propellers. As the propellers push air backward, the plane shoots forward. The faster the air is pushed back, the faster the plane moves ahead. A jet plane moves forward by pushing hot gasses backward.

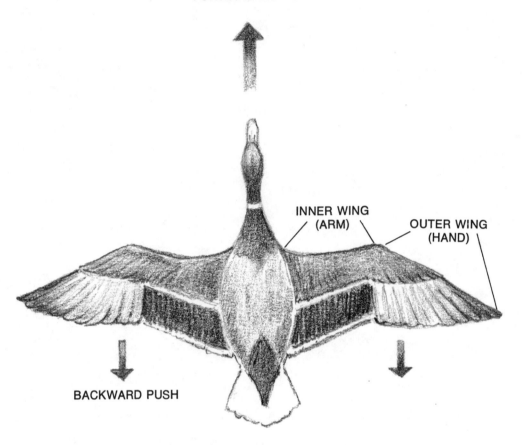

FORWARD MOTION

INNER WING
(ARM)

OUTER WING
(HAND)

BACKWARD PUSH

A bird can move forward by flapping its wings. As the wings beat up and down, the inner wing, or arm, does not move much. This part of the wing works just like the outstretched wing of a plane. It supplies the lift that holds the bird up. Most of the flapping is done by the outer wing, or hand, where primary flight feathers beat against the air. These flight feathers work like a plane's propellers. They push air backward, driving the bird forward.

29

On the downstroke, the wings move forward and down.

flight feathers closed for the downstroke

A bird's flight feathers overlap each other. When the bird pulls its wings down, the flight feathers snap shut, like slats closing in a Venetian blind. Now the wings are almost airtight. They can push with great force against the air.

Primary flight feathers push backward against the air
like propellers, driving the bird forward.

The downstroke is the power stroke. With each downward wing beat, the bird drives itself forward. As the tightly closed wing comes down, the inner wing moves only a little. The outer wing, or hand, sweeps *forward and downward* toward the bird's head. The primary flight feathers bite into the air like small propellers. Each flight feather twists sharply and pushes backward against the air as a propeller does.

flight feathers opened for the upstroke

When the bird pulls its wings up, the flight feathers snap open, like slats opening in a Venetian blind. With the feathers spread apart, air passes easily through the wings. This makes it easier for the bird to raise its wings.

32

Air passes through the opened flight feathers
as the bird's body shoots ahead.

The upstroke does not provide much forward power. A bird pulls its wings up mainly to get them back into place for the next downstroke. Now the wings sweep *upward and backward,* away from the bird's head. The flight feathers still push against the air, but not as strongly as before. By the end of the upstroke, the bird's body has pulled ahead of its wings. An instant later, the wings start moving forward and downward again.

Gliding Flight

When a bird is moving forward fast enough, it can stay in the air without flapping its wings. It simply spreads its wings and *glides* easily along. The bird is being pulled downward by the earth's gravity. At the same time, its wings are holding it up because of lift. The bird drops toward earth very slowly, as though it is sliding down a hill of air.

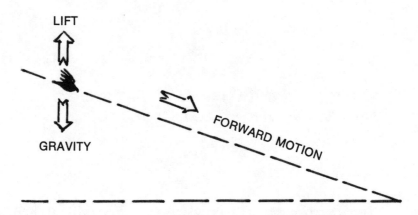

Gliding is the simplest kind of flight. A paper glider moves forward and downward as a bird does. An airplane glides as it coasts to a landing. The first animals to glide were probably early ancestors of birds. Millions of years ago, these creatures would climb to the top of a tree or cliff. They would spread their primitive wings, jump into space, and glide toward earth.

herring gull gliding

The best gliders are birds with large wings. Large wings have more lifting power than small ones. The more lift a bird has, the longer it can glide before it has to beat its wings again. Gulls, eagles, vultures, and albatrosses spend most of their time gliding. They can travel for miles with scarcely a movement of their wings. Small birds can glide short distances between wing flaps. A tree swallow beats its wings to gain speed, then glides to rest its muscles, then beats its wings again.

Soaring Flight

Andean condor soaring

Soaring is a special kind of gliding. When a bird glides in still air, it moves downward as well as forward. But when it soars, it is swept upward by a rising current of air, as though it is being lifted by an invisible elevator.

One type of rising air current is called a *thermal,* which means "heat." As the sun beats down, heated air boils upward from the ground. Huge, doughnut-shaped bubbles of warm air may rise thousands of feet into the sky. Soaring birds spread their wings and circle above these warm air bubbles. The rising air carries them higher and higher.

bald eagle soaring

obstruction current

Another kind of rising air current is caused by strong winds blowing upward. When the wind hits a mountainside or building, it is forced to blow over it. This is called an *obstruction current*, and it offers many soaring birds a free ride.

WIND

dynamic soaring

Sea birds use ocean breezes when they soar. An albatross can travel miles this way. It glides swiftly downward, swept along by the wind, until it almost reaches the water. By this time it has picked up enough speed to turn sharply and zoom upward like a roller coaster. Then it turns again and starts another downward glide. This is called *dynamic soaring.*

Taking Off

Taking off is hard work. If a bird does not get off to a fast enough start, its wings will not lift it into the sky. All birds flap their wings harder than usual to gain speed when they take off. Even a powerful jet plane must roar down the runway until it has picked up enough speed to leave the ground.

As a bird takes off, it usually heads into the wind. Suppose the wind is blowing at 10 miles an hour. Even though the bird is standing still, air is already rushing past its wings at 10 miles an hour. This gives the bird a headstart. Taking off in calm air is harder, because the bird must reach full flying speed under its own power. Airplanes also take off into the wind.

40

*common heron
taking off into wind*

A ring-billed gull works up speed for the takeoff by running across the sand and flapping hard.

A stork catapaults itself into the air by pushing away from the ground with its long legs.

A duck pushes against the water with its large, webbed feet.
It patters quickly across the surface until it gains flight speed.

A large bird like an eagle tries to land atop cliffs or trees.
When it is ready to take off again, it simply leaps into space.

43

Steering

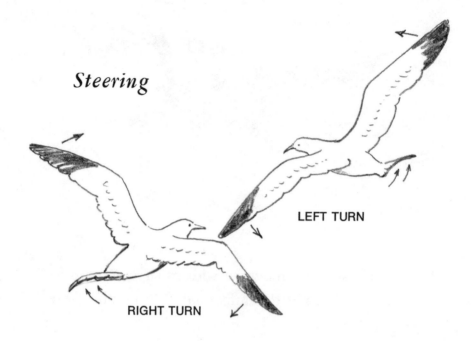

LEFT TURN

RIGHT TURN

A bird steers with its wings and its tail. If the bird wants to turn right, it lowers its right wing and raises its left wing. It flaps the left wing harder. The left wing moves forward faster, while the right wing falls behind. The bird's body swings around to the right.

The bird's tail also helps it turn. The tail can be opened and closed like a fan. As the bird begins its right turn, it spreads its tail wide. Then it twists the tail up on the right side and down on the left. Air speeding past the bird pushes against the tail and helps swing the bird's body around. To turn left, the bird twists its tail in the opposite direction. Birds with large tails can turn sharply at high speeds. Birds with small tails cannot steer nearly as well.

44

GOING UP

COMING DOWN

When the bird wants to move upward or downward, it uses its wings and tail again. To climb higher, it tilts its wings up in front and flaps them harder so it will have more lift. At the same time, it bends its tail up. Air rushing over its body pushes down against the raised tail. The rear of the bird goes down while the head goes up, just like a seesaw.

To move downward, the bird bends its tail down. Air rushing under its body pushes up against the tail. Now the rear of the bird goes up while the head goes down. At the same time, the bird tilts its wings down in front and doesn't flap as hard. The wings lose some of their lifting power. The bird levels off, or heads downward. When a bird dives, it folds its wings against its body and drops like a missile.

Landing

Landing is the most dangerous part of flying. When a bird gets ready to land, it must slow up. If it comes in too slowly, its wings will lose all their lifting power, and the bird will crash to the ground. If it comes in too fast, it can injure or kill itself. All birds land as slowly as possible.

First the bird slows its wingbeats, just as a landing plane slows its propellers. Then it heads into the wind and glides toward earth with its wings spread. Close to its landing target, the bird tilts its wings up and opens its wing slots to keep from stalling. It spreads and lowers its tail, which acts as a brake. It also lowers its legs and pushes them forward. Just before landing, the bird cups its wings like two parachutes and fans the wings back and forth. This acts as another brake. Finally the bird reaches out with its feet and touches down.

46

bluebird

When a songbird lands on a branch, its legs bend at the joints like shock absorbers.

albatross

Birds that land on the ground often run to a stop.

ring-necked duck

The easiest place to land is on water. A duck comes in fast, pushes its webbed feet forward, and skids to a stop.

Different Wings for Different Purposes

By looking at the size and shape of a bird's wings, you can often tell how the bird lives.

Short, rounded wings are a clue that the bird lives in woods, shrubs, or underbrush. Small songbirds that perch on branches have short, rounded wings. They can dart and twist through trees and bushes without hurting themselves. Stubby wings are also found among many birds of the forest and among ground-feeding birds like woodcocks and quail. These birds can turn sharply in tight places. They can make quick escapes by flapping hard and fast for short distances, but they cannot fly fast for very long.

goshawk

white-throated sparrow

bobwhite

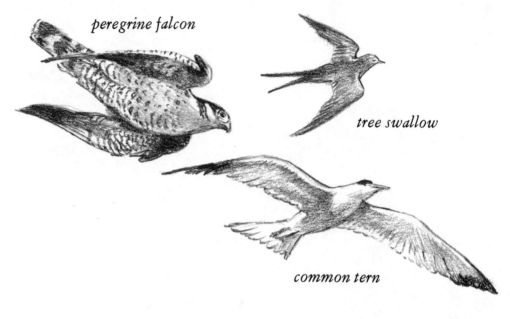

peregrine falcon

tree swallow

common tern

Long, pointed wings mean that the bird lives in open country or near the sea. These birds are fast fliers. They sweep through the sky, often snatching their food out of the air. High-speed wings are found among land birds like falcons, swallows, and swifts; among shore birds like sandpipers and plovers; and among most birds that migrate long distances.

blackfoot albatross

The biggest wings belong to birds that glide and soar much of the time. Sea soarers, like gulls, shearwaters, and albatrosses, have very long, narrow wings with sharp tips. They sail along with the winds. Land soarers, like eagles, hawks, and vultures, have very wide wings with deep slots in the wing tips. The slots prevent stalling as the birds circle slowly overhead.

vulture

pin-tailed duck

Fast and Slow Flappers

You can always tell how big or small a bird is by the speed of its wingbeats. Since small wings have less lifting power than big ones, small birds must flap quickly, while large birds can flap more slowly. A vulture beats its giant wings about once a second. Each stroke drives the vulture forward with great force. Medium-sized birds like ducks and crows flap two or three times a second. A sparrow beats its stubby wings about 14 times a second, while the smaller chickadee flaps 25 times a second. Of all birds, hummingbirds are the smallest. A ruby-throated hummingbird beats its tiny wings about 70 times a second. Hummingbirds get their name from the humming sound made by their rapidly beating wings.

vulture
1 wingbeat a second

crow
3 wingbeats a second

chickadee
25 wingbeats a second

hummingbird
70 wingbeats a second

Hummingbirds: Hovering Flight

A hummingbird's wings work differently from those of other birds. The wings are shaped like stiff paddles. They move only at the shoulders, where they swivel freely in almost any direction. This makes it possible for a hummingbird to *hover,* or "stand still," in the air as it sips nectar from a flower. While hovering, it keeps its body upright. As its wings sweep forward, they twist sharply toward the ground and push air

downward (see drawing above). As the wings sweep back, they flip over. Now the top of each wing faces the ground and again pushes air downward (see drawing below). The wings act like the whirling rotor of a helicopter, which also drives air downward. Besides hanging motionless in the air, a hummingbird can fly straight up and even backward, which no other bird can do.

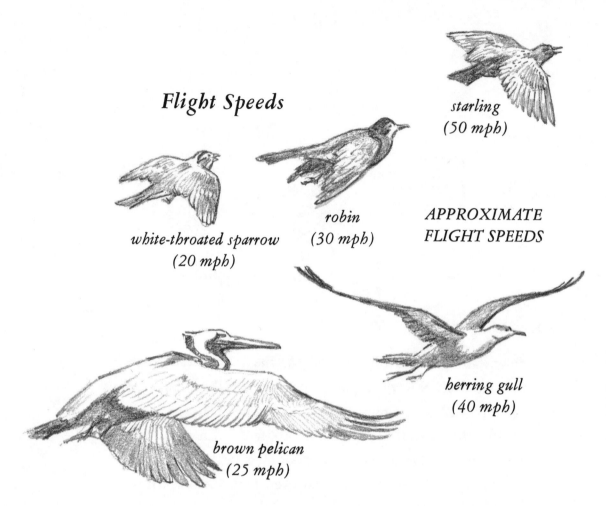

Flight Speeds

starling
(50 mph)

robin
(30 mph)

*APPROXIMATE
FLIGHT SPEEDS*

white-throated sparrow
(20 mph)

herring gull
(40 mph)

brown pelican
(25 mph)

A bird's flying speed depends partly on where the bird is going. A sparrow cruises along at 15 or 20 miles an hour. When it heads home to roost, it may speed up to 25 miles an hour. If it is chased by an enemy, it can fly 35 miles an hour. Its speed is also affected by the wind. When the bird flies with the wind at its tail, it gets an extra push from behind. If it turns around and heads into the wind, it passes more slowly over the ground.

mallard duck
(65 mph)

peregrine falcon
(100 mph)

racing pigeon
(80 mph)

Canada goose
(60 mph)

Indian swift
(up to 200 mph)

Flight speed depends mainly on the design of a bird's wings. Songbirds with short, rounded wings normally fly between 15 and 25 miles an hour. Swallows and starlings use their long, pointed wings to fly 40 or 50 miles an hour. Ducks and geese reach speeds of 60 miles an hour or more. The fastest birds are probably falcons and swifts, whose wings sweep back like those of a jet. A peregrine falcon, or duck hawk, can approach 100 miles an hour. The speed record for level flight is held by an Indian swift, which was clocked at the amazing speed of 200 miles an hour.

We humans have watched birds fly for thousands of years. Until recent times, we knew little about what happens when a bird speeds through the air. High-speed photography gave us our first close-up look, revealing birds in flight as they had never been seen before.

Today we are studying flying birds with the aid of motion pictures, wind tunnels, electronic computers, and mathematical formulas. The flapping wings of a bird, with their millions of twisting and bending parts, are far more complicated than the rigid wings of any aircraft. We know more about bird flight than our ancestors even suspected. But we still don't understand everything that happens when a bird beats its wings and takes to the sky.

Glossary

airfoil　Any surface, such as a wing, that is designed to produce lift when a bird or plane moves through the air. An airfoil usually has a curved and streamlined shape.

air sacs　Large, bubble-like spaces filled with air, attached to a bird's lungs and branching throughout its body. Air sacs reduce a bird's weight and help cool its body as it breathes.

alula　A group of three to six small, stiff feathers attached to the movable thumb in front of a bird's wing. When the alula opens, it forms a narrow slot. Air squeezing through the slot speeds up as it flows over the wing.

angle of attack　The angle at which a wing, or other airfoil, meets the oncoming air. As the front of the wing tilts upward, the angle of attack increases, causing air to flow faster over the wing.

barbs　Thin, hairlike strips that extend from the central shaft of a feather. The barbs of a contour feather are held together by microscopic hooks (called barbules and barbicels) and form the web, or vane. The barbs of a down feather have no hooks and sprawl about in all directions.

contour feathers　Large, stiff feathers that cover a bird's body and provide its streamlined shape. Contour feathers in the wings are called flight feathers.

down feathers　Small, fluffy feathers that are the first body covering of baby birds and form a warm undercoat in many adult birds.

dynamic soaring　Using ocean breezes to glide downward and then soar upward again and again in almost endless cycles.

60

flapping flight   The most common kind of bird flight, in which the power for forward motion is supplied by the up-and-down movement of the wings.

flight feathers   Long contour feathers in the wings that are used for flight. The wide contour feathers in the tail are also important in flight.

flight muscles   Large, powerful muscles, attached to the breastbone, that raise and lower a bird's wings.

gliding   The simplest form of flying, in which forward motion is supplied by the pull of gravity while lift is supplied by outstretched wings. Gliding flight requires no movement of the wings.

hand section   The outer part of a bird's wing, extending from the wrist to the wing tip. The hand section, with its primary flight feathers, pulls the bird forward as the wing flaps.

hovering   A special form of flapping flight, used mainly by hummingbirds, in which the bird beats its wings rapidly and suspends itself in midair.

inner wing   The part of a bird's wing that extends from the elbow to the wrist. The inner wing supplies most of the lift that keeps a bird in the air.

keel   The large breastbone, which anchors a bird's flight muscles.

lift   The force that holds a bird or plane in the air. Lift results from air pressure beneath the wings and suction above the wings.

obstruction currents   Rising air currents, used by soaring birds, which are caused by strong winds blowing upward over buildings, mountainsides, and other obstructions.

outer wing   The part of a bird's wing that extends from the wrist to the wing tip; also called the hand section.

primaries   Long flight feathers attached to the hand sections, or outer wings. Primaries act as the bird's "propellers," providing forward thrust as the wings flap.

quill   The hollow base of a feather, located at the end of the central shaft. The quill is fastened to the bird's skin.

secondaries   Flight feathers attached to the inner wing, or forearm, between the wrist and elbow. Secondaries pad the wing and provide the airfoil shape that lifts a bird.

shaft   The stiff central stem of a contour feather.

slotting   A technique used to make air flow faster over the top of a bird's wing. Narrow slots are formed by opening the alulas in front of the wings, or by spreading flight feathers at the wing tips. Air squeezing through these slots speeds up as it flows over the wing.

soaring   A special form of gliding flight, in which a bird spreads its wings and is swept upward by rising air currents. Like gliding, soaring requires little or no movement of the wings.

stalling   The sudden disappearance of lift above a wing. Stalling occurs when air no longer flows smoothly over the wing top but breaks away and swirls around. If a bird or plane stalls, it starts falling.

tertiaries   Wing feathers attached to the elbow and upper arm, filling the gap between the bird's body and its main flight feathers.

thermals   Large bubbles of warm air that rise thousands of feet into the sky, carrying soaring birds upward.

webs   The thin, flat sections of a contour feather on either side of the feather's central shaft. Webs, also called vanes, are made up of hundreds of barbs.

Index